Original title:
Beneath the Weight of Whispered Worries

Copyright © 2024 Creative Arts Management OÜ
All rights reserved.

Author: Elias Montgomery
ISBN HARDBACK: 978-9916-90-576-0
ISBN PAPERBACK: 978-9916-90-577-7

Shadows of Concern Dancing in Silence

In twilight's grasp, shadows creep,
Whispers of worries, secrets we keep.
A heart heavy, burdened with fears,
In the silence, a symphony of tears.

Echoes of doubt weave through the night,
Flickering hopes, dimming the light.
Faces worn, shadows dance near,
In the silence, we harbor our fear.

Yet in the stillness, a spark may rise,
Bringing forth strength beneath the skies.
With every breath, a chance to mend,
In the silence, we find our own end.

So let us face what shadows may bring,
With courage borne from the depths within.
For even in silence, we are not alone,
In the shadows, the seeds of hope are sown.

The Soft Sigh Within the Heart

In the silence, whispers play,
Gentle dreams weave through the day.
A rhythm soft, a pulse so low,
Unseen love, like rivers flow.

In shadows cast, where feelings hide,
Embers glow, they do not bide.
Each heartbeat speaks, a tender song,
In quiet moments, we belong.

Crumbling Walls of Quiet Despair

Brick by brick, the shadows creep,
Memories haunt, they're hard to keep.
Faded hopes, like dust, remain,
Each heartbeat echoes lost in pain.

Once sturdy walls, now worn and cracked,
Silent cries that time has packed.
Whispers of joy, now faint and thin,
In the ruins, where dreams begin.

Whispered Fears in the Dark

Beneath the moon's soft silver hue,
Fears take shape in shadows, too.
Haunting thoughts that swirl around,
In whispered breath, no safety found.

A heart that trembles, eyes that close,
The dark reveals what no one knows.
Each flicker sparks a silent dread,
In the night, where dreams seem dead.

Muffled Voices Beneath the Stars

In the night, soft echoes rise,
Voices blend beneath dark skies.
Stars above, like candles glow,
Illuminating paths we know.

Silent words that drift and tease,
Carried forth by gentle breeze.
We hear the whispers, feel the call,
In our hearts, we find it all.

Glistening Tears of Silent Struggles

In shadows cast by doubt's cruel hand,
Glistening tears fall on barren land.
Hopes unlocked in whispered dreams,
Silent struggles lost in screams.

Each drop a story, each sigh a plea,
Carved in silence, yet screams to be free.
Boldly they shine, though the heart feels strain,
Glistening tears, signs of pain.

Treading Water in Shallow Streams

Feet submerged in waters so light,
Treading softly, avoiding the fight.
Bubbles rise from laughter and grief,
Shallow streams conceal deep belief.

With every step, the current flows,
Treading water where stillness grows.
The ripples whisper of dreams untold,
In shallow streams, a heart grows bold.

The Unraveled Threads of Fragile Peace

Threads once woven in harmony's grace,
Begin to fray, lose their rightful place.
A tapestry torn by time's cruel tease,
The unwrapped stories, fragile peace.

Whispers of hope now tangled in doubt,
A world confused, searching for a route.
Yet in this chaos, resilience grows,
From unraveled threads, strength will expose.

Still Waters Run Deep with Fear

Calm surfaces hide a tempest's roar,
Still waters run, yet they yearn for more.
Beneath the hush, a tremor breeds,
Silent whispers turn into deeds.

Fear lurks deep in the quiet's embrace,
While shadows dance in a hidden space.
Yet courage finds a way to appear,
In still waters, confront the fear.

Whispers in the Wind of Worry

In shadows soft, a murmur calls,
With every breeze, the heart enthralls.
A gentle tug, a hint of dread,
In whispered tones, the worries spread.

Beneath the stars, a secret sigh,
As moonlight fades, the thoughts comply.
Each rustle stirs the quiet mind,
In silence deep, the fears unwind.

Lurking Beneath Layers of Fear

Beneath the surface, shadows creep,
In stillness, silent secrets seep.
Veils of doubt begin to form,
A quiet storm, a fierce alarm.

The echoes dance in darkened halls,
A heart that races, softly falls.
Yet through the haze, a glimmer shines,
In layered depths, the strength entwines.

Murmurs of Tension in Twilight

As day concedes to evening's grace,
A tension thrums in quiet space.
The twilight hums a wistful tune,
While shadows blend with the rising moon.

Between the light and growing night,
A fragile peace, then fears take flight.
In each heartbeat, the whispers soar,
A reminder of what lies in store.

The Veil of Unseen Pressures

A weight unseen, a heavy cloak,
In silence binds, no word is spoke.
Beneath the calm, the currents pull,
The world feels vast, yet strangely small.

With every breath, a subtle strain,
A fight for peace, a quest through pain.
Yet through the veil, a spark ignites,
A chance to rise, to claim new heights.

Heavy Hearts in Hushed Moments

In the quiet glow of dusk,
Love's whispers softly tread.
Heavy hearts weigh down the trust,
As silence fills the thread.

Eyes meet with a shy glance,
Words linger on the tongue.
Heavy hearts dance in the chance,
For fears have come undone.

Emotions rise like the tide,
Lost in a world unknown.
Heavy hearts no more can hide,
Fractured dreams overthrown.

Yet in the dawn's embrace,
Hope flickers, faint but true.
Heavy hearts can find their place,
With love's light breaking through.

Shadows Cast by Lingering Doubts

In the corners of the mind,
Doubts drift like fading smoke.
Shadows twist, they curl and bind,
As every silence spoke.

A question lingers in the air,
Echoes of what's unsaid.
Shadows stretch beyond compare,
Where trust once gently tread.

In the dim light of the soul,
Fears weave a tangled net.
Shadows dance, they lose control,
Hopes caught in cold regret.

Yet still the heart will fight,
To break away the night.
For in the dawn's first glow,
Shadows fade, and courage grows.

Unraveling the Tapestry of Concern

Threads of worry intertwine,
In a fabric worn and frayed.
Unraveling patterns, so divine,
    Confessions yet delayed.

Color fades from every seam,
As whispers turn to cries.
Unraveling the fragile dream,
With every truth that lies.

Each knot holds a hidden tale,
Stitched in the heart's retreat.
Unraveling fears, they pale,
As honesty takes its seat.

And through the tangled threads of grief,
A strength begins to bloom.
Unraveling the flawed belief,
From shadows into room.

The Weight of Secrets Left Unshared

In the depth of night we keep,
Secrets tucked away like dreams.
The weight of shadows, buried deep,
In silence, pain redeems.

Heavy thoughts like stones will rest,
On souls too burdened to fly.
The weight of secrets, unconfessed,
Leaves hearts too scared to try.

Yet whispers long to find a voice,
To lift the heavy shroud.
The weight of truth can be a choice,
To be seen, to be loud.

In courage soft as morning light,
Together, we can share.
The weight of secrets, lost from sight,
Brings freedom from our care.

The Silent Symphony of Inner Strife

In shadows deep, thoughts intertwine,
The echoes of dreams, a bittersweet sign.
Melodies clash in the quiet of night,
A symphony played without any light.

Strings gently tug at the heart and the soul,
A dance of despair takes its toll.
Whispers of hope drown in the fray,
Yet still, the silence guides my way.

Ghosts of Anxiety in the Night

Soft whispers call from the corners of thought,
Ghosts of anxiety linger, overwrought.
Eyes wide open, yet sleep fades away,
Haunted by shadows that silently sway.

A breath caught deep, like a whispered dare,
Ghosts brush my shoulder, their cold, empty stare.
In this long night, fears take their flight,
Chasing the dawn, retreating from light.

Unseen Chains of My Mind

Invisible links bind my restless dreams,
Ties made of worry, harsh and extreme.
With every thought, they pull and they strain,
A struggle within, a tempest of pain.

In silence, they govern the paths I can't tread,
A prison of doubts where the brave fear to tread.
Yet in the stillness, I seek to unbind,
To break these chains that shadow my mind.

Paths Wrought with Unacknowledged Tensions

Along the paths where silence reigns,
Unseen tensions weave through the strains.
Every step echoes with tales untold,
A journey of shadows, both timid and bold.

Underneath layers of calm and serene,
The weight of the world lies sharp and unseen.
Yet in this chaos, a whisper takes flight,
Guiding my heart to confront the night.

Threads of Worry Woven Through Time

In shadows deep, the thoughts entwine,
Each moment threads a heavy line.
A tapestry of doubt unfolds,
In silent whispers, the past scolds.

The clock ticks on, no rest in sight,
Each worry weaves through day and night.
Yet hope, a stitch, breaks through the seam,
A fragile thread, the heart's soft dream.

Through tangled fears, we search for light,
A pattern shifts; we hold on tight.
The fabric of our lives does sway,
In woven strands, we find our way.

Though threads may fray and colors fade,
The story is one we've bravely made.
In every twist and turn we find,
The strength to weave a love that's blind.

The Weight of Silent Sighs

In quiet rooms, where echoes lie,
The weight of words becomes a sigh.
Each breath held tight, a story told,
Of dreams once bright, now bittersweet gold.

The moments pass, like drifting smoke,
In silence, heavy, hearts provoke.
What's left unsaid, a burdened chain,
In shadows deep, we bear the strain.

The world spins on, but here we stand,
With unvoiced hopes and trembling hands.
Each sigh a sound, though small it seems,
A quiet chant of fractured dreams.

Yet in each breath, a chance to breathe,
To mend the heart, to dare, believe.
The weight may linger, but we rise,
With strength to cast aside our sighs.

Dances of Disquiet in the Mind's Eye

In chambers vast, where shadows flow,
Thoughts twist and turn in silent show.
A dance of doubt, a silent waltz,
Each step reveals our hidden faults.

The music plays but fades away,
In restless dreams, we lose our way.
Yet in the chaos, sparks ignite,
A flicker of truth breaks through the night.

The mind's eye paints with colors bold,
A story only we have told.
With every twirl, we find our place,
Amidst the disquiet, we embrace.

Though shadows loom, we'll take the stage,
With every breath, we turn the page.
In dancing still, we find our peace,
The mind's eye whispers, fears release.

When Silence Speaks Louder Than Words

In quietude, the heart concedes,
A share of thoughts that silence breeds.
With heavy hearts, we stand apart,
Where silence speaks, it breaks the heart.

No words to cloak the yearning gaze,
In stillness, longing softly plays.
A glance exchanged, the truth revealed,
In unspoken bonds, our wounds are healed.

Each breath a weight, each pause a plea,
In tranquil spaces, we are free.
With silence woven through the night,
Our souls find solace in the light.

For oftentimes, the quiet reigns,
Beyond the noise, where love remains.
When silence speaks, emotions stir,
In wordless moments, we can confer.

Veils of Concern in Twilight's Embrace

In the dusk, shadows blend and sway,
Whispers of worry wander astray.
The colors fade, a gentle retreat,
As fears in the silence softly meet.

Beneath the veil, secrets keep tight,
Dreams shrouded in the coming night.
In twilight's arms, doubts intertwine,
Anxiety's dance, an unyielding sign.

Stars flicker, like thoughts in despair,
Drawing the heart into burdens to bear.
A twilight hush, heavy and true,
Veils of concern, an endless view.

Yet dawn will break, with hope in its beam,
Casting away the shadows that teem.
In the light, worries begin to flee,
And strength finds its voice to set us free.

Secrets Cradled in the Quiet

In the stillness where silence resides,
Secrets hide, like the ebbing tides.
Thoughts wrapped in whispers, soft and tight,
Cradled gently in the blanket of night.

Moments unfold in the dimmest glow,
A treasure trove hidden, only we know.
Words left unsaid linger in air,
Promises nestled in tones of despair.

Time tiptoes past on cushions of gray,
Yearning to speak, yet lost in the fray.
Every heartbeat, a plea in disguise,
Echoing softly, love never dies.

In this quiet, connections still thrive,
Breathless truths, we strive to contrive.
In these secrets, the heart is alive,
Cradled in comfort, where feelings arrive.

Murmurs of Hesitation in the Dark

In the shadows where whispers creep,
Murmurs of doubt awake from deep.
Each silence begs for a voice to rise,
Masked by the night, hidden in sighs.

Footsteps falter on uncertain ground,
Questions linger, no answers found.
In the pitch, imaginations spark,
Fueling the fears that linger in dark.

A heartbeats drum, a fragile sound,
Dancing with echoes that wrap around.
Hesitation clouds the path ahead,
Casting a veil where hope has fled.

Yet within the void, the faintest light,
Guides the lost through the thickest night.
In every pause, courage can bloom,
Transforming the whispers that breed their gloom.

The Gravity of Unvoiced Apprehensions

In the still air, tensions abound,
Unvoiced feelings cling to the ground.
Their weight feels heavy, a silent strain,
Pulling the spirit like drops of rain.

Eyes may wander, but words stay locked,
Echoing hearts that remain unshocked.
Tiny tremors of thoughts unshared,
Tethered in worry, the soul feels bare.

Each pulse throbs with stories untold,
Yearning for courage to break the mold.
A dance of emotions, pushed deep inside,
Gravity pulling where fears reside.

Yet in that pull, there's strength to find,
A voice to rise, unbind the mind.
From shadows of doubt, we learn to soar,
Unvoiced apprehensions, no more ignored.

Webs of Worry in the Silence

In the corners of my mind, they weave,
Fragile threads of what I believe.
Each whisper grows, a fearful sound,
Within the silence, worries abound.

They tangle tight, these webs of dread,
A constant stream of thoughts unsaid.
In shadows cast by fleeting light,
I search for peace in the endless night.

Yet hope may shine, a distant spark,
A guiding flame through the dark.
With every breath, I'll break these chains,
And leave behind my silent pains.

A Journey Through Labyrinths of Doubt

In corridors of shifting fears,
I wander lost through tangled years.
The walls of doubt close in so tight,
Each step I take feels far from right.

Voices echo, calling me near,
Fueling every hidden fear.
Navigation's hard; the path obscured,
Yet every twist feels strangely lured.

I seek the truth that lies within,
Past shadows thick where doubts begin.
A journey fraught with trials to face,
Yet still I chase that hopeful place.

Shadows, Secrets, and Silent Sighs

In the depths where shadows creep,
Secrets lie, and silence weeps.
Each sigh a story left untold,
In echoes faint, the heart turns cold.

Beneath the weight of hidden fears,
Whispers linger, haunting years.
A dance of ghosts in moonlit glow,
While memories fade, the shadows grow.

Yet through the gloom, a light may gleam,
A fragile flicker of a dream.
With courage kindled, I will rise,
And cast aside the darkened skies.

The Knot of Unexpressed Concerns

Tied in knots, my thoughts reside,
Unexpressed, they swell inside.
Each worry twists, each fear renews,
A tangled mass of endless blues.

Silent burdens weigh me down,
A hidden frown beneath the crown.
With every glance, the world appears,
A veil of whispers, cloaked in tears.

Yet if I breathe and dare to speak,
Perhaps this weight will start to leak.
With words released into the air,
I'll find the strength to truly share.

Walking the Tightrope of Unshed Tears

On a flickering line we tread,
Balancing dreams with silent dread.
Each step whispers tales of strife,
Caught between stillness and life.

Waves of emotion crash and sway,
Yet we choose to hold the fray.
In the quiet, strength might grow,
As we wander to and fro.

With every heartbeat, choices rise,
Facing shadows with weary eyes.
A delicate dance, we embrace,
As hope lingers in this space.

Voices Distilled from Distant Storms

Echoes drift from the past,
Whispers of troubles amassed.
Across the void, they call to me,
Carrying tales of what could be.

In the thunder, truths collide,
Memories crashing like the tide.
Yet within chaos, a song is spun,
Melodies birthed from battles won.

Silent screams from ages old,
Each note a story to be told.
From the tempest, voices rise,
Stirring the calm with thunderous sighs.

Suns Behind Clouds of Concern

Hidden rays in a churning sky,
Hopes await where shadows lie.
Cautious light seeks to emerge,
Breaking forth with quiet urge.

Each day dawns with uncertain ease,
Fleeting moments carried by breeze.
Yet as clouds begin to part,
Warmth can mend a weary heart.

Underneath the weight we bear,
Lies a promise, bright and rare.
For every storm that steals our sight,
Suns await to reignite.

Silent Shadows of Unspoken Fears

In the corners, doubts reside,
Whispered worries we can't hide.
Each shadow plays a quiet role,
Echoing the depths of the soul.

Lingering in the still of night,
Softly crafting our fright.
The unsaid fills the empty space,
A haunting dance we cannot face.

Yet in silence, strength can grow,
From the shadows, light can flow.
A journey forged through dark and light,
Finding courage in the night.

A Symphony of Disquietude

In shadows deep, the echoes play,
A haunting tune that drifts away.
Each whispered note, a fragile thread,
Woven dreams, now left for dead.

The restless night, a weary sigh,
As stars above begin to cry.
Silent screams in the moon's pale light,
Awake the heart, ignite the night.

Life's dissonance, a fleeting chance,
To find the peace in chaos' dance.
Yet in the storm, I seek the calm,
A soothing balm, a whispered psalm.

And still I yearn for solace found,
In melodies of love profound.
Though echoes fade, the heart will sing,
In symphonies of everything.

Weights That Anchor the Heart

Heavy lies the heart's burden,
With chains unseen, yet none more certain.
Each worry cast, a stone in place,
Building walls, my own embrace.

In quiet moments, doubts arise,
Each flicker dims, and hope just sighs.
These weights we bear, a cost to know,
For love, for loss, for joy's soft glow.

Yet in the depth, resilience stirs,
The soul's quiet strength, amidst the slurs.
Like roots that grip the earth so tight,
We find our ground, we find our light.

With every test, we learn to rise,
Beyond the weight, we touch the skies.
For anchored hearts, though bound to ache,
Will learn to bend, and not to break.

The Unraveled Threads of Anxiety

Frayed edges whisper tales untold,
A tapestry of fear, bold yet cold.
Each thread unwinds, a story lost,
The warmth retreats, I count the cost.

In moments dark, when shadows creep,
The mind a labyrinth, too deep to sleep.
Thoughts collide like storms at sea,
Unraveled dreams come haunting me.

Yet in the chaos, glimmers shine,
A fragile hope, a simple sign.
That through the fray, we weave anew,
With threads of strength, a brighter hue.

So in the end, I'll find my way,
Through tangled paths, towards the day.
For every fear, a lesson learned,
In the heart's embrace, the fire burned.

Softly Spoken Fears in Darkened Corners

In quiet rooms where shadows play,
The unvoiced fears begin to sway.
Each soft gasp a secret told,
A weight unseen, yet heavy, bold.

Muffled whispers haunt the night,
In corners dim, they seek the light.
The heart's quiet dread, so subtle,
With every pulse, the silence cuts little.

Yet even in despair's tight grip,
A flicker sparks, ignites the trip.
Through fog and mist, I seek to find,
The strength within, in heart and mind.

For softly spoken fears may tire,
But in their wake, I find my fire.
To face the dark, with courage near,
And turn the whispers into cheer.

Weightless Yet Heavy: An Invisible Load

A burden unseen, it lingers near,
Whispers of worry, echoing fear.
Floating like feathers, yet pulling me down,
In silence I wear this invisible crown.

Moments of peace, they flicker and fade,
Caught in a cycle where choices are made.
A delicate balance, this life that I bear,
Weightless yet heavy, a constant affair.

Through laughter and tears, I tread a fine line,
Searching for solace, a moment divine.
The heart and the mind in a constant debate,
Weightless yet heavy, I carry my fate.

In shadows, the truth sometimes hides in the dark,
Hiding the pain, suppressed like a spark.
Though weightless I drift, I know deep inside,
This invisible load is a ghost I can't hide.

The Labyrinth of Troubling Thoughts

In corridors twisting, my mind takes a flight,
Chasing the echoes that linger at night.
Each turn, a reminder of dreams left behind,
The labyrinth deepens, I'm losing my mind.

Walls built from doubt, like shadows they creep,
Whispers of worries that fracture my sleep.
Around every corner, a riddle to face,
The path that I'm on, seems a lost race.

Yet through the confusion, I seek out the light,
A glimmer of hope in the darkest of night.
With every wrong turn, I gather my strength,
In this maze of thoughts, I'll find my own length.

So onward I wander, for wisdom I crave,
In the heart of the labyrinth, I'll learn to be brave.
Each thought, a lesson, each tear, a release,
Navigating the maze, I'll strive for my peace.

Gossamer Threads of Introspection

Threads of reflection, so fragile and fine,
Weaving the fabric of moments in time.
Each thought a junction, a path to explore,
In whispers of stillness, I search for the core.

Silken and soft, they shimmer with grace,
Painting the edges of every place.
Gossamer dreams float on whispers of air,
Echoing secrets that dare me to care.

With every connection, I stitch and I mend,
The tapestry growing, its colors transcend.
In silence, I gather the threads of my mind,
Gossamer voices, the wisdom I find.

So gentle the touch, yet so vivid the hue,
Each moment a thread, weaving life anew.
Caught in this web, my heart learns to feel,
Gossamer threads of the truths I reveal.

Whispers in the Twilight of Doubt

In the twilight of doubt, shadows begin,
Whispers of fear creep under my skin.
Where light starts to dim, and the echoes play,
I question the path I travel each day.

Voices like breezes, they stir in the night,
Sowing confusion, obscuring the light.
What if I falter? What if I stray?
In the twilight of doubt, will I find my way?

Yet within the shadows, a flicker remains,
A spark of resilience that battles the chains.
I gather the whispers, transform them to strength,
In the twilight, my spirit will go to great length.

With courage as armor, I'll face my own fears,
Each whisper a lesson that softened my tears.
Through twilight, I see, amidst doubt's cruel fight,
The whispers guide me, and I find my light.

Storm Clouds Over Calm Horizons

Dark clouds gather in the sky,
Whispers of thunder looming nigh.
Beneath the calm, a tension swells,
Nature's warning, a tale it tells.

The horizon glows with shades of gray,
Yet sunlight fights to hold its sway.
Winds will shift, the storm will break,
In this dance, the skies awake.

Raindrops patter on thirsty ground,
A symphony in chaos found.
With every flash, a pulse, a roar,
Life's rhythm echoes, evermore.

As calm retreats, the storm will reign,
Washing away the silent pain.
In tempest's heart, we find our way,
Through storm clouds rising, we will stay.

The Pressure of What Remains Unsaid

Words linger heavy on the tongue,
In shadows deep, they remain unsung.
A silent truth, a hidden plea,
Bound in silence, longing to be free.

In every pause, a world appears,
Filling silence with hidden fears.
Unspoken thoughts, a weight we bear,
Echoes of love hang in the air.

Each glance exchanged, a story told,
In yearning hush, our hearts unfold.
What lies beneath the surface bright,
Is woven deep in the silent night.

To share our hearts, a daring quest,
Yet, oftentimes, we choose the rest.
But in that hush, we learn to stay,
To cherish what we cannot say.

Caged Hearts in a Whispering World

In shadows cast, hearts beat alone,
Behind the bars of fears we've known.
Whispers float on winds so light,
Dreams entangled in the night.

We wear our cages made of doubt,
While silent screams long to break out.
In crowded rooms, we feel unseen,
Caged in thoughts that paint us mean.

Yet through the cracks, a light may seep,
A chance for souls to wake from sleep.
With gentle words, the bonds may fray,
And hearts can learn to dance and play.

In a world that whispers low and clear,
May courage rise, replacing fear.
For in our hearts, the strength to soar,
Awaits the moment we choose to explore.

Threads of Worry Weave the Heart

Threads of worry tangle tight,
Weaving patterns out of sight.
In the loom of anxious thought,
Peace escapes, happiness sought.

Moments lost in webs we spin,
Fearing all that lies within.
Each thread pulls, a heavy weight,
In silence, dreams dissipate.

Yet in the loom, a chance may rise,
To weave with hope beneath the skies.
To take the fears and fashion art,
Transforming worry to a hopeful start.

So let us stitch with threads of light,
A tapestry of dreams in sight.
For though the heart may bear its load,
With love, we lighten every road.

A Canvas Stained with Quiet Turmoil

In hues of grey, the colors blend,
Frayed edges whisper tales untold.
Beneath the surface, emotions mend,
A heart encaged, yet bold.

Brush strokes heavy, a silent plea,
Each mark a tremor, a distant ache.
A portrait formed, yet hard to see,
In shadows deep, the vows we break.

Crimson flashes, a memory's flare,
While muted tones lead thoughts astray.
In this artwork, a secret pair,
Of joy entwined with shades of gray.

From every corner, turmoil streams,
Yet beauty lies within the strife.
A canvas formed from broken dreams,
Reflects the chaos of our life.

Ripples of Repressed Reflections

In tranquil waters, shadows play,
Waves of thoughts just below the skin.
Every ripple hints at the gray,
Of battles lost, the weight of sin.

Thoughts emerge like whispers soft,
Echoes of a life lived in haste.
Dancing lightly, yet soaring aloft,
Memories linger, not meant to waste.

Beneath the calm, the tempest brews,
Each reflection a sigh, a part.
In the stillness, the truth imbues,
A heart confined, yet longing to start.

So may these waters clear in time,
Reveal the treasures held so dear.
Through the ripples and quiet rhyme,
We find ourselves, we shed the fear.

Weighty Echoes of Silent Sorrow

In hushed rooms, the echoes resound,
Heavy whispers that bind the soul.
Each silence deepens, a shattering sound,
A longing heart loses control.

Beneath the surface, sorrow lies,
Wrapped in shadows, cloaked in night.
Unseen tears weave through the skies,
Drifting dreams, out of sight.

Every heartbeat, a ghostly chime,
Marking hours that slip away.
In each moment, we catch the rhyme,
Of heavy burdens we cannot sway.

Yet in these echoes, strength may grow,
From pain arises a tender grace.
In silent sorrows that ebb and flow,
We find the light, a warm embrace.

Chasing Shadows of Lingering Thoughts

In twilight's glow, shadows entwine,
Hints of memories flicker and fade.
Chasing whispers along the line,
Where dreams are born, and fears invade.

Every thought, a shadowed thread,
Tugging softly at the mind's design.
In this maze where silence led,
We search for truth, we seek the sign.

Yet still the shadows dance and play,
Elusive forms that slip away.
In every corner, they softly sway,
A haunting echo of a brighter day.

So let us chase these wisps of night,
For in their depths, the dawn may gleam.
Through every shadow, we find the light,
A gentle path to guide our dream.

Surrendering to Subtle Storms

Whispers in the evening air,
Gentle breezes, soft and rare.
Clouds that gather, dark and fleet,
Nature's symphony, bittersweet.

Raindrops dance on window glass,
Moments fleeting, like blades of grass.
The heart opens to a sigh,
As shadows stretch beneath the sky.

Trees sway lightly, branches bend,
Embracing change, we must attend.
In quietude, the storms unfold,
Lessons in the warmth of cold.

And so we yield to nature's plea,
Let currents guide us, wild and free.
Surrendering to subtle dreams,
Where silence breathes, and comfort beams.

Veiled Voices of Quiet Dread

Softly creeping through the night,
Uneasy shadows steal the light.
A haunting tune, a distant call,
Voices echo in the hall.

Whispers hide behind closed doors,
Filling minds with silent wars.
Each thought a mirror, cracked and bent,
Reflecting fears we can't prevent.

In solitude, the heart does race,
Chasing phantoms, a lost embrace.
Veils of doubt like fragile lace,
Shroud the truth of our own space.

Yet in this fog, a spark might bloom,
Courage found amidst the gloom.
Facing echoes, we stand bold,
Voices rise, their tales retold.

The Invisible Burden of Thought

Weightless notions drift and glide,
In the cavern where dreams reside.
Thoughts like shadows, swirling deep,
Secrets hidden, none to keep.

Battles waged within the mind,
No one sees what we must bind.
Layers thick with cares untold,
Emotions writ in shades of gold.

Beneath the calm, a turmoil brews,
Carrying burdens we can't refuse.
In silence, echoes form and swell,
Waves of sorrow, tales we tell.

Yet in this weight, we find our grace,
Moments of stillness, our embrace.
Invisible chains may weigh us down,
But through the struggle, we're profound.

The Suffering Beneath the Surface

A mask we wear, a practiced smile,
Hiding trials that stretch a mile.
Underneath, the currents churn,
In the shadows, lessons learn.

Tides of pain, both sharp and sweet,
Whispers of fear that can't compete.
Yet in the depths, a strength awaits,
To rise again, despite the weights.

In silence, we gather our scars,
Mapping journeys to distant stars.
The pain we hold, a sacred art,
Binding souls, connecting heart.

So let us lay our burdens down,
Embrace the truths, wear them proud.
For in the suffering, we find our song,
Together, we're where we belong.

Silent Cries Beneath the Surface

In shadows deep, whispers lie,
Echoes soft, a muted sigh.
Hearts conceal what they can't show,
Silent cries where no one goes.

Beneath the calm, a tempest brews,
A world unseen, colored in blues.
The longing stirs, yet hides away,
Words unspoken in wild ballet.

Masks we wear in everyday light,
Hiding storms that rage at night.
Behind the smile, a tear may burst,
Silent cries that quench the thirst.

But in the dark, hope starts to gleam,
A faint light caught in distant dream.
For every cry beneath the skin,
A spark remains, a chance to win.

The Weight of Thoughts Unseen

Weights unseen, they weigh me down,
A heavy heart in a crowded town.
Whispers swirl in my restless mind,
Searching for peace that's hard to find.

Each thought a stone, each worry a chain,
Building a tower of quiet pain.
In the silence, they clamor and clash,
Breaking the calm with an urgent flash.

Yet in the stillness, I find a way,
To sift through shadows, to greet the day.
The weight grows lighter with each soft breath,
As hope unfurls its wings from death.

Embrace the thought, let it take flight,
Release the tension, bask in the light.
Though burdens cling and doubts may roam,
Within my heart, I'll carve a home.

Gentle Burdens in the Quiet Night

Under the stars, the world feels slow,
Gentle burdens in soft moon's glow.
The night carries secrets, soft and sweet,
Whispers of dreams where silence meets.

In shadows deep, I lay my head,
Thoughts of tomorrow weave in my bed.
A gentle sigh escapes my lips,
As the night wraps me in its flicks.

Each twinkling star, a wish that's made,
Casts a light on worries that fade.
In the calm of night, I find my muse,
Gentle burdens, I choose to refuse.

Tomorrow comes with its urgent demands,
But here in the night, peace gently stands.
I'll cradle my thoughts, let them take flight,
For tomorrow blooms from this quiet night.

The Murmur of Worry's Caress

A whisper soft, a gentle sweep,
Worry's caress, as shadows creep.
Thoughts entwined like tendrils of vine,
Choking dreams that once did shine.

In corners dim, the echoes call,
A symphony of doubt, a silent thrall.
Close to the heart, worries take root,
Nurtured by fear, they grow and shoot.

Yet gentle breezes ease the fret,
With every breath, I seek to forget.
A quiet voice says, 'Let it be,'
In the murmur, I find my key.

For in the noise, there's wisdom's song,
A way to right where I feel wrong.
In the caress, I learn to trust,
Embracing worries, turning them to dust.

In the Company of Fearful Whispers

In the dark where silence reigns,
Shadows flicker, tightening chains.
Voices murmur, secrets unwound,
Echoes of dread in silence found.

Tread softly on the haunted ground,
Fear's numb grip, a haunting sound.
With every step, a heartbeat quick,
In whispers cloaked, the world feels thick.

A shiver runs down, spine to heel,
What lurks out there remains concealed.
In twilight's grasp, we hold our breath,
Fearful whispers tease of death.

Yet hope ignites, a flickering light,
Through dread's embrace, we seek the fight.
In company of whispers frail,
Together we stand, we will prevail.

The Sorrow of Solitude's Echo

In a room where silence breathes,
Solitude weaves its silent wreaths.
Lonely shadows dance with grace,
In this empty, forgotten space.

Time lingers with a heavy sigh,
Windows weep as days drift by.
Heartbeats echo, soft yet clear,
A symphony of longing near.

Every corner holds a memory,
A gentle ghost, a silent plea.
Within these walls, the past remains,
In solitude's arms, love wanes.

Yet in the stillness, hope resides,
For in each echo, a heart abides.
Through sorrow's veil, we glimpse the dawn,
In solitude's echo, we carry on.

Hidden Cries Beneath a Calm Surface

Beneath the facade, still waters flow,
A tempest brews where few would know.
Hearts disguise their deepest fears,
While laughter masks the silent tears.

Wind whispers tales of unspoken pain,
A surface calm, but souls in strain.
In crowded rooms, we wear our masks,
Yet solitude to truth still asks.

Ripples form as secrets churn,
Hidden cries, for justice yearn.
Through veils of calm, storms reside,
In silence where our truths collide.

Yet still we hope for love's bright ray,
To break the chains and guide our way.
For beneath the calm, we rise and sing,
Embracing joy that healing brings.

Shadows Cast by Lingering Thoughts

In the twilight, shadows play,
Lingering thoughts in disarray.
Flickering images drift and sway,
Chasing dreams that slip away.

Each whispering doubt, a thief in the night,
Stealing peace, dimming the light.
With every breath, a haunting trace,
Of memories lost in time and space.

As moonlight dances on haunted walls,
Echoes of wonder in silence calls.
In shadows cast by fleeting dreams,
Hope twinkles softly, or so it seems.

Yet within this dance of dark and light,
We find the strength to face our plight.
For shadows may linger, but hearts stay bright,
In the vast embrace of the starry night.

The Heavy Cloak of Secret Woes

In shadows deep, where whispers dwell,
The burdens weigh, too hard to tell.
A cloak of gloom wraps round the heart,
Each thread a secret, torn apart.

The nights are long, the silence loud,
In heavy fog, the sorrows shroud.
Unseen battles, fought alone,
In every sigh, the pain is grown.

With eyes like glass, we mask the pain,
Yet deep inside, there's just disdain.
The heavy cloak, we wear with pride,
Hides the tears we've never cried.

But in the dawn, a light may spark,
A chance to lift the heavy dark.
With courage found, we rise anew,
And shed the cloak, embrace the true.

Fragile Minds and Unraveling Threads

In fragile minds, thoughts drift and sway,
Like autumn leaves that fade away.
A tapestry of doubts and fears,
Unraveling gently through the years.

With every strand, a story spun,
Of battles lost and webs undone.
Yet in the chaos, hope does gleam,
A whispered promise, a vivid dream.

Our hearts hold strong, though threads may fray,
In imperfections, we find our way.
We stitch the pieces, one by one,
And find the strength to face the sun.

Through tangled paths, we learn to cope,
In fragile minds, we weave our hope.
With every tear, a lesson learned,
In unison, our spirits burned.

The Silent Scream of Grown Worry

In shadows cast, the quiet screams,
A weight that haunts our waking dreams.
The world moves on, yet we stand still,
With every heartbeat, growing chill.

Our thoughts collide in endless strife,
In silence lingers haunting life.
The worry grows, a silent beast,
In restless nights, it finds a feast.

We wear our masks, the smiles bright,
But hide the storm, the inner fight.
With every glance, a fear concealed,
A battle fought but never healed.

Yet in the dark, a glimmer gleams,
A fragile hope that breaks the seams.
With every dawn, might come a way,
To hush the screams, to seize the day.

Shadows Looming Over Lighted Paths

On lighted paths, the shadows creep,
A dance of doubt, a secret keep.
Each step we take, the darkness near,
In bright of day, we still feel fear.

The sun may shine, yet shadows grow,
In every heart, a silent woe.
They stretch and bend, obscure the view,
Of dreams we chase, of skies so blue.

Yet through the dusk, a voice will call,
To rise again, to stand up tall.
Defy the shadows, let hope soar,
For every path leads to a door.

In every light, there's shadow's trace,
But courage guides us through that space.
With every step, we find our way,
And face the dusk to greet the day.

Beneath the Calm

The surface glimmers soft and bright,
A peace that wraps the heart so tight.
Yet deep below, the shadows sway,
A dance that's hidden from the day.

The silence hums a quiet song,
With secrets held, where dreams belong.
In tranquil depths, the truth may hide,
A weight of choices, deep and wide.

Beneath the calm, the waters churn,
For every tide, a lesson learned.
In every ripple lies a tale,
Of silent storms that softly scale.

Yet in the quiet, hope can rise,
To sail beyond the cloudy skies.
And though the depths may twist and roam,
Within the calm, we find our home.

A Quake of Uncertainty

The ground beneath begins to shake,
A shiver runs with every break.
Where once was sure, now veils of doubt,
In whispered winds, the fear breaks out.

A tremor's thought, it grips the mind,
Each moment lost, so hard to find.
The cracks in plans spread far and wide,
While echoes of the past collide.

What once seemed stable, now unsure,
Unraveling threads, it seeks a cure.
Through shifting sands, we search for ground,
As chaos reigns, no peace is found.

Yet in the quake, there lies a call,
To rise again, to stand up tall.
For every fall needs strength anew,
Through uncertainty, our paths break through.

Ghostly Whispers in the Dark

In shadows cast by fading light,
Soft murmurs drift into the night.
A haunting sigh, a chill in air,
The echo of a whispered prayer.

Through corridors of time we stroll,
While memories weave with heart and soul.
The past encroaches, sweet and near,
As phantoms rise, they disappear.

Beneath the canopy of stars,
The silent echoes speak of scars.
Each voice a tale of love and loss,
In spectral dance, we bear the cross.

Yet in these whispers, truth remains,
A bond that lingers through the pains.
For even though they fade away,
The ghostly sounds will always stay.

Invisible Storms of the Mind

Thoughts rage like tempests in the dark,
Invisible, they leave a mark.
A whirlwind spins with no escape,
From silent fears that shape our fate.

Perceptions twist like shadows cast,
The present fades, the future vast.
In every gust, a doubt resides,
A storm within that often hides.

Yet amidst the chaos, sparks of light,
Brighten the corners of the night.
A glimmer of peace may still arise,
In quiet moments, wisdom lies.

So sail through storms with heart held high,
For even clouds must one day fly.
The mind may churn, but hope will bind,
The tides of thought, our strength designed.

The Silent Weight of Crippled Dreams

In shadows cast by broken plans,
Lay dreams unrealized in shaky hands.
A longing heart, it aches in vain,
For paths not taken, lost to pain.

The quiet toll of nights spent cold,
With whispers of the dreams once bold.
Each thought a weight, unmovable,
In silence clings, unshakeable.

Yet hope may flicker, faint and shy,
Like distant stars, they still can fly.
For in the depths of endless night,
A flicker can ignite the light.

So let us mourn what might have been,
But also seek what lies within.
For dreams may wane, but hearts remain,
To find new ways and heal the pain.

Anxious Waves Lapping on the Shore of Thought

The sea retreats with heavy sighs,
Lapping gently, like whispered cries.
Thoughts collide like waves at dusk,
Fleeting moments, lost in husk.

Tides of worry ebb and flow,
Drawing fears that loom and grow.
Each ripple stirs a tempest near,
An ocean vast, where doubts appear.

Footprints mar the sandy shore,
As fleeting thoughts are lost in roar.
Echoes linger in the foam,
A restless mind, it lacks a home.

Yet slowly, as the stars align,
Calm descends, a gentle sign.
For every wave that once came wild,
Peace can flourish, tender and mild.

The Unfolding of Clouded Visions

In the haze where dreams reside,
Blurred reflections often hide.
Clouded thoughts, like autumn leaves,
Drift away, as silence weaves.

Layers part to find the light,
Waking visions, bold and bright.
What was lost now finds its grace,
In the heart, a sacred space.

Each moment offers paths anew,
With clarity, the soul breaks through.
What once seemed a daunting maze,
Transforms into a brighter gaze.

Step by step, the fog retreats,
Opening up, the world greets.
In the light, my spirit soars,
Through the veil, a heart explores.

Echoes of Stress Amidst Serenity

In quietude, a whisper grows,
Beneath the calm, the tension flows.
Rhythms pulse in hidden ways,
Stressful echoes, haunting days.

Like shadows dance on sunlit floors,
Anxieties press on opened doors.
Stillness sings its soothing song,
Yet beneath, the fears belong.

Respite found in nature's hold,
Whispers soft, both fierce and bold.
Yet with each breath, I hold the noise,
Striking chords of silent joys.

To balance storms with tranquil skies,
Finding peace as chaos flies.
An inner calm, a strength to glean,
Through echoes, I embrace the serene.

In the Shadow of Unseen Burdens

Shadows linger, heavy cloak,
Silently weaving tales bespoke.
Unseen burdens rest on hearts,
Weighing down, like fractured parts.

Yet within the veil of night,
Hope unfurls in cautious light.
Each step taken, though unsure,
Leads to paths that might endure.

The weight can teach, the dark can guide,
In the silence, fears subside.
With every breath, resilience grows,
From unseen depths, the spirit flows.

In shadows deep, there blooms a spark,
Illuminating every mark.
Through burdens carried, strength is gained,
In unseen battles, freedom claimed.

Hushed Cries of the Burdened Spirit

In shadows deep, where whispers dwell,
A spirit cries, but none can tell.
The weight of silence, heavy sighs,
In corners dark, the burden lies.

Through cracked facades, the truth will creep,
In the night's embrace, a soul will weep.
Yet in the depths, a flicker glows,
A flickering flame that gently flows.

Held captive by the chains we wear,
In echoes soft, we find despair.
But still we rise, though shadows bite,
With whispered dreams, we chase the light.

So hush those cries, let courage swell,
For buried hope will break the spell.
With every step, the spirit roams,
In hushed tones, it finds its home.

Navigating the Fog of Hidden Fears

In twilight realms where shadows blend,
I wander lost, where fears descend.
The mist entangles, cloaks my heart,
From dreams I forged, now torn apart.

Each step I take, a whisper low,
A voice within that ebbs and flows.
Through veils of doubt, I strain to see,
What lies beyond this entity.

Yet in the haze, a beacon calls,
Through labyrinths of silent brawls.
With trembling hands, I seek the shore,
To face the fears, forevermore.

So through the fog, I will persist,
With every chance, I'll coexist.
For in the dark, a spark resides,
And there, the journey truly guides.

The Weight of the Unsaid on Our Souls

Beneath our breath, the words remain,
In quiet spaces, echoes pain.
The unspoken bonds that tie us close,
A heavy shroud, a silent ghost.

Each glance unveils the truth we hide,
In every heart, a soft divide.
Yet longing lingers in the air,
A testament of soul laid bare.

With clenched fists, we guard the flame,
Afraid to whisper, call a name.
The weight of unsaid fills the night,
A burden borne, obscured by fright.

But still I dream of words unchained,
In hopes that love will be sustained.
What lies between us, shall we share?
In honest light, dissolve despair.

Quiet Reflections in a Turbulent Sea

In tempest nights, the waters churn,
Yet in the storm, my heart will learn.
The waves may crash, the winds may howl,
But still I stand, unfolding my scowl.

Through chaos fierce, a truth unveiled,
A whisper soft, where dreams have sailed.
In quiet depths, I find my peace,
A solace found, where troubles cease.

The ocean's roar, a symphony,
In every note, I feel the free.
Each wave that breaks, a story told,
In quiet strength, my spirit's bold.

So here I drift, in ebb and flow,
Among the stars, my heart will grow.
In turbulent seas, I'll sail with grace,
And find my light in nature's embrace.

Silent Shadows of Somber Thoughts

In the quiet corners, shadows creep,
Whispers of memories, secrets to keep.
Flickering candles, dimming the light,
Echoes of dreams that fade into night.

Heavy is the heart that bears the weight,
Silent confessions wrapped in fate.
A tapestry woven with threads of despair,
Softly they linger, suspended in air.

In the stillness, a voice that won't rise,
Chasing the ghosts beneath whispered skies.
Footsteps retreating from paths not trod,
Searching for solace, seeking the nod.

Yet through the shadows, a flicker remains,
A glimmer of hope within the pains.
Retrace the echoes, remember the sighs,
Silent shadows may bring forth new skies.

Echoes of Unspoken Fears

In the hush of night, fears are laid bare,
Whispers of doubt linger in the air.
Shadows of worry dance on the wall,
Each unvoiced thought, a challenging call.

The heart beats faster, caught in the fray,
Silence amplifies what words cannot say.
Eyes cast downward, avoiding the light,
Echoes surround me, a palpable fright.

What ifs linger, tangled in the mind,
Hesitation grips, leaving peace behind.
In the corners of my soul, there's a fight,
Braving the dark, searching for the bright.

Yet in the quiet, strength can be found,
Facing the shadows, breaking the ground.
Voices may tremble, but courage is near,
Step by step forward, confronting the fear.

The Burden of Unvoiced Anxieties

A heavy mantle drapes over my soul,
Burdened by thoughts that constantly toll.
In the depths of silence, worries take flight,
Unstated fears cloaked in the night.

The mirror reflects a mask, not my face,
Trapped in a cycle, I yearn for grace.
Each sigh a whisper, each glance a plea,
Heartbeats echo the weight, longing to be free.

Yet hope flickers amidst the shade,
Threads of resilience, a choice to be made.
In the hush of despair, courage can sow,
Unvoiced anxieties can learn to grow.

Taking a step, embracing the day,
Lifting the burden, come what may.
For within this struggle, strength shall emerge,
Unvoiced no longer, I rise from the verge.

Gossamer Threads of Hidden Doubts

Delicate whispers dance on the breeze,
Gossamer threads bind like soft, silent keys.
In the tapestry woven, doubts find a way,
Flickering flames that threaten to sway.

Each question unasked pulls gently at seams,
Fraying the fabric of long-held dreams.
With bated breath, I wade through the mist,
Searching for answers that just can't exist.

In twilight's embrace, shadows intertwine,
Hidden fears surface, clearly defined.
Yet in the depth of this intricate weave,
Strength lingers quietly, daring to believe.

For woven in doubt are threads of delight,
Brightening the gloom with potential insight.
As I unravel, the journey takes shape,
Gossamer threads, my fears to escape.

Echoes of Unrest in Midnight Dreams

Whispers linger in the dark,
Restless thoughts ignite a spark.
Shadows dance upon the wall,
Silence answers every call.

Fractured visions weave and twist,
In the void, the dreams persist.
Fragments of a haunted past,
Holding tight, they fade so fast.

Crescendo rises, fears collide,
In twilight's grip, we must confide.
Echoes linger, softly plead,
In midnight dreams, our souls are freed.

Yet dawn will break this shaky realm,
Illuminating thoughts at helm.
Awakening from veils of night,
We chase the dreams that shine so bright.

The Burden of Thoughts Left Unsaid

In crowded rooms, I wear my mask,
Hiding truths, an arduous task.
Words once sharp, now dulled by fear,
Lingering doubts I hold so near.

Promises unvoiced, hearts untouched,
In silence binds where love is clutched.
Each unspoken thought weighs me down,
A hidden crown, a lover's frown.

Time slips by like sand through hands,
Holding tight to dreams that strand.
Yearning for the chance to speak,
Longing hearts, so tired and weak.

Regrets loom large in twilight's sigh,
In the stillness, we wonder why.
Yet hope remains, though shadows cast,
To find a way, to break the fast.

Cloaked in Gentle Anxieties

Softly cloaked in worries slight,
Chasing comfort through the night.
Dreams entwined with whispered fears,
I gather strength through fallen tears.

Waves of doubt crash on the shore,
Anxiety's grip—an endless chore.
Yet in the dark, a light does gleam,
Hope emerges, a fragile dream.

Clocks tick by with burdens spun,
Heartbeats echo, weary run.
In every pause, a thought takes flight,
Searching for solace in the night.

Through tangled thoughts, I seek my way,
Finding peace in dawn's soft ray.
With every breath, I stand my ground,
In gentle calm, my strength is found.

The Hidden Tides of Lingering Doubts

Underneath the surface lies,
Waves of doubt that rarely rise.
They pull and push within my mind,
A silent storm, so undefined.

Questions swirl like autumn leaves,
Trusting moments, yet it grieves.
In this sea, I search for light,
Navigating through the night.

Thoughts retreat, then surge again,
Moments lost in fear's domain.
Yet in the depths, I might just find,
A strength within, a love unconfined.

As tides recede, I make my stand,
Embracing all that life has planned.
In hidden depths, I learn to swim,
Against the tide, I rise and grin.

Portraits of Unseen Strain

In quiet rooms where shadows crawl,
The weight of silence starts to call.
Behind the eyes, a storm may brew,
A portrait formed, yet never true.

With smiling lips and laughter bright,
A hidden war becomes the fight.
Each heartbeat echoes, deep and loud,
In crowded spaces, lost in crowd.

Fingers tremble, hands held tight,
In gentle frames, the heart feels slight.
Each breath a sigh, each glance a plea,
What lies beneath, we seldom see.

Yet in this veil, strength finds its way,
Resilience grows, come what may.
Through unseen strain, a light will beam,
A quiet warrior's steadfast dream.

The Dance of Shadows and Frets

In flickered light, shadows take flight,
They twist and turn, both soft and slight.
A waltz of whispers, fears collide,
In silence deep, where worries hide.

Each movement speaks of battles fought,
In the darkness, solace sought.
A step too far, a breath too near,
The dance reveals what hearts might fear.

With every sway, the weight appears,
Frayed edges cloak unspoken fears.
A symphony of heartache plays,
In shadows cast, the spirit sways.

Yet through the night, hope stirs and gleams,
In rhythm found, we chase our dreams.
With shadows close, we learn to cope,
In the dance of hearts, we find our hope.

Echoes of Turmoil in Solitude

In corners dim, where echoes dwell,
Silent screams weave a hidden spell.
Each thought reverberates like a stone,
In solitude, we're never alone.

The clock ticks slow, each second weighs,
Memories plague like the foggy haze.
In the stillness, turmoil ignites,
Whispers of battles that none ignites.

Faces flash, a haunting parade,
Past joys and sorrows, memories fade.
Yet through the dark, light starts to creep,
In echoes deep, new dreams we keep.

For in this silence, strength is found,
Amidst the chaos, our hearts resound.
Through turmoil's grip, we learn to feel,
In solitude, we start to heal.

Beneath Fragile Smiles, a Heavy Load

A cheerful grin, a crafted face,
Yet burdened hearts, a hidden space.
Behind the laughter, stories hide,
In fragile smiles where tears abide.

Each moment bright, a fleeting game,
While inner struggles roar like flame.
The weight we carry feels so vast,
Yet still we play, we wear the mask.

With woven threads of joy and pain,
The tapestry reveals its strain.
Beneath the surface, darkness creeps,
Where secrets dwell, and silence weeps.

But in such depths, we find our grace,
In heavy loads, we learn to trace.
For every smile has a story told,
Of strength and courage, brave and bold.

Milton Keynes UK
Ingram Content Group UK Ltd.
UKHW022116251124
451529UK00012B/548